RHYME AND

THE ETERNAL

Reflections on the Divine

By Josephine M. Woods

a Kiwi in Yorkshire

First published in Great Britain as a softback original in 2014

Copyright © 2014 Josephine M Woods

The moral right of this author has been asserted.

Typeset in Baskerville and Baskerville Old Face

Editing, design and publishing by UK Book Publishing

UK Book Publishing is a trading name of Consilience Media

www.ukbookpublishing.com

ISBN: 978-1-910223-18-5

REORDER – if not available through retail outlets please contact Josephine –
josephine.m.woods@gmail.com

Contents

Acknowledgments

To the *Holy Tradition*

both *East* and *West*

To

My *Mum*, whose compassion and care for everybody
she knew was such a good example;

My *Dad* for introducing me to The Path;

My *wonderful husband* who is such a great partner to tread this path
with and whose hard work and enthusiasm has kept this project alive.

Author's Note

All references to The Eternal Spirit as '*He*' etc can also be substituted with '*It*' or '*She*' or '*I*' or '*God*', etc.

Introduction

In May 2010 a New Zealand retired Primary School
teacher and her husband moved to live in Corn Mill,
a quiet cul-de-sac on the outskirts of Menston, a small
village some 12 miles north west of Leeds.

Facing east and nestled at the bottom of the western flank of the
Chevin Hill, the flora, fauna, wildlife, weather and seasons provide
the location for 'A Kiwi in Yorkshire's Reflections on the Divine'.

Since arriving in the UK in 2005 – first to Scotland then Yorkshire
– she has written several book series: this anthology; picture books
for younger children; fantasy series for girls; adventure space series
for boys; and an illustrated series of stories of New Zealand birds.

The Eternal is the second anthology in the poetry series Rhyme
and Reason following The Transient, published August 2014.

e-books, talking books and large print are also
being considered for publishing.

I'm Here

I'm here! I'm closer than a prayer!
I'm breathing in your breath.
I'm waiting here.

Around you in the universe
And watching from within
If all could stop life's busyness
And stop mind's constant din.

I'm here within, above, below
I'm here, I'm through and through.

No need to think.
No need to plan.
I'm all you need that's True.

I am the 'Silence' in your heart.
I was there at your birth,
The very start of your life
– Here on Earth.

All through your life I'm watching
Each tiny step you take.
I show MySelf in moments
When you are most awake.

So meet Me in the Silence
And then I'll take you home.
Please meet Me in the Silence,
No more you'll have to roam!

Then as your life moves onwards
Towards its final breath,
I'll meet you at that moment
When you come to life's death.

I am the Life!
I am the Way!
Remember this from day to day.
Return as often as you may,
To Me!
To Rest!
To Peace!
Then in your life My Love will be
For it will never cease,
Till to Me you will finally come!
To Me, that Truth, the only One.

For I am You
And You are Me.
Here in the Now,
Eternally.

There – light and love and peace you'll find
To nourish and give peace of mind.
Now and forever in Infinity.

Inspired by the words of Desmond Tutu

Divine Presence at Dawn

I am the sound of the babbling brook.
I am the scent on the breeze.
I am the first glow of light at dawn
That silhouettes hills and trees.

I am the sound of the tinkling chimes.
I am the silence so still.
I am the voice that speaks these rhymes,
That come to me as Your Will.

I am the taste of the tea in the cup.
I am what is perceived.
I am all the movements within and without.
All that which is believed.

The time before dawn is so precious,
It heralds the entrance of day.
That silence at dawn is so precious,
Giving strength to proceed on the Way,
Giving guidance to practise and pray
So in His Presence we'll stay.

The World

We are – addicted to, afflicted by the world.
Oh to meditate and contemplate
And find the bliss within,
But thoughts and feelings in our minds
They set up such a din.

We are – addicted to, afflicted by the world.
The family ties that make us sigh,
The many doubts and whims.
We want to live, we want to die,
They make us laugh, they make us cry
And then at last we wonder why,
We are – addicted to, afflicted by the world.

Then in the silence, there we find
Some solace and some peace of mind.
So mind be still and meditate
And in our hearts let's contemplate
The reason why we're here.
No longer then we'll fear
Being – addicted to, afflicted by the world.

Wondering

I wonder why we wonder why?
We wonder all day long
Why this? Why that?
This constant chat,
This never ending song.

The mind perceives this universe,
It's always on the go.
The mind it grasps this universe,
It always wants to know
Why this? Why that?
It wonders on and on
And on and on and on.
So stop: then watch
And just enjoy the show.

At Home with Me

Stay at home with Me in your heart
And I will give you peace.
Stay at home with Me in your heart,
Your constant roaming cease.
Stay at home with Me in your heart
Where it is silent and still.
Stay at home with Me in your heart
For that is My Own Will.

If you stay home with Me in your heart
Then you will feel no pain.
If you stay home with Me in your heart
In Me you'll always reign.
Come home to Me again.

Your Voice

The body, heart and mind,
They feel so full of strife
When one is always caught up
In the ocean of this life.

The problem is that
There is such belief
That all of this is real
So, full of grief
We suffer in this life which
Is so brief.

But then I hear your voice
Below the ocean's storms
This voice that calls one inward
And gradually my heart warms.

There is such comfort
In those depths
Of silence and such peace.

Your voice, so real
That all the other surface
Noises cease.

Just like that candle in
The windless sanctuary where it burns.
My heart and mind keep listening,
For only You they yearn
As your voice magnifies
And penetrates all fear,
Then shines its light
Within the heart,
As closer one draws near.

So finally sound and listener –
They are one.
No more the dark cave.
Now there is just sun.

The Creator

The Creator of this world
Has made it for his sport
And with his consciousness and love
This world he doth support.

Then as the ages they unfold,
Beginning with the age of gold
To silver, bronze, then iron age,
Where many wars around us rage,
He watches this great show.
He knows where it will go
From very start to very end
When all again in Him will blend
And merge and come to rest.

And so He watches all unmoved.
He need have no concern
And we like Him unmoved should be.
It's this we have to learn
For life is death and death is life,
We need not strive and suffer strife
Though in the midst of pain.

For though the clouds course through the sky
And bring much wind and rain,
In time the clouds they finally clear
And there's the sun again.

Our lives are like the ages.
This world, it is our stage.
Our Creator knows our script
From start to its last page.
Thus He will keep on watching
And supporting us each day.

It's His Will we are acting out,
So struggle though we may,
We might as well get on with it
And just enjoy the play.

The Quiet Voice

Desires, they shout so loudly.
Thus reason, shining clear
Is only heard in silent mind
Beyond all doubt and fear.

Its gentle, quiet whisper
'Tis often hard to hear
When all our thoughts
Are clamouring. They cry, "Please hold us dear!"

But when in Meditation
Our mind and heart are still,
We hear that voice of reason,
That voice of His true will.

So listen in the silence!
So listen in the space!
Where Truth within
And Truth without
Will soon come face to face.
Pervading... every place.

Listen

"I'm here.
I'm closer than a prayer",
Around you in the Universe
Around and through and through.
There is no they;
There is no them;
There is no me and you.
Remember this...
For this is what is true.

I'm here, around,
In every sound,
So listen to my song.
All life it plays my symphony,
So listen all day long.
'Tis when our thoughts
Go round and round
That we feel small and dark and bound
And then we do not hear
My harmony in all things
Loud and clear.

"Those who have ears to hear
Let them hear."

Inspired by the words of Desmond Tutu

The Watching – Part One

The world is like a photograph
With negative behind
Developed by the great Māyā*
And witnessed by Mankind.

From rest comes forth the movement,
The play it thus unfolds
Displayed by light of consciousness
For us all to behold.

But who is it perceiving
Through every ear and eye?
Through every sense perception?
The One that we call 'I'.

Great Time appears to travel on
Through birth, decay and death,
But I who am the Timeless
Supports with Prāna's** breath.

Stay seated in the watching.
Rest in the great Ahum***.
But don't forget that all this play
Is all just My Great Fun.

Ref
Māyā – Sanskrit – Illusion of this world
**Prāna – Sanskrit – Life giving force*
***Ahum – Sanskrit – The One called I*

The Watching – Part Two

The next step when we're watching
Is to know it's everywhere.
It's not just sitting
Watching in this body sitting here.

Existence is a sense
We have when mind's at rest in peace.
Existence it is everywhere
And it will never cease.

Shown by the Great Existence
Is the mighty Lord Ahum*,
With Buddhi** and its reasoning power,
A shining like the sun.

That radiant light of consciousness
That lights all we perceive.
It's shining always everywhere
And it will never leave.

Although the aging body
Decays and finally dies.
This light, this mind, this reasoning lives on,
Through all it lies
Supporting all, pervading all
Through multifarious lives.

Ref
* - Ahum – Sanskrit – The One called 'I'.
** - Buddhi – Sanskrit - intellect; the faculty of discrimination

The Mirror

The world is like a mirror.
The glass it is a screen
Of consciousness on which
We watch the ever changing scene.

The background of the mirror
Reflects the silvery show,
It is unseen and yet reveals
This pageant that we know.

This drama it unfolds and moves
Through life until its end
And then it merges back again
And into life's source blends.

So what's behind the mirror?
So what's behind life's dream?
We need to know
As things are not quite really as they seem.

Life's Journey

All we need to do is clear the screen
On which Māyā* paints her illusory dream.
For there we'll find the Truth
We really know.
The peace, the love, the light that is just so.

That living, vibrant Essence,
Sure and still.
The intelligence that doth reveal His Will.
Its needs appear before us every day.
We need to follow –
It will show the way.
Then step by step
Unfolding and providing all we need
To know and do,
So thus we may proceed.

Then day by day
With Him we are more filled.
A place in His heart for us each He'll build
And there eternally
Thus – we'll be fulfilled.

Ref
Māyā – Sanskrit – Illusion of this world

The Source

From the Source comes the force
That lets us perceive.
From the Source comes Knowledge;
No more need to 'believe'.

From the Source comes the light
That makes all things bright,
It even continues
Through world's darkest night.

From the Source comes Existence
We're aware of from birth,
Which supports us through life
As we live here on Earth.

From the Source comes contentment,
So deep and so still.
From the Source come the Laws
That engender His Will.

So rest in that Source,
It is where we belong.
It's the artist, the singer,
The writer, the song.

And when we return
Every night into sleep,
It's that Source that we enter,
That Source that's so deep;
Where all our projections,
They all disappear.
No more stress.
No more strife.
No more doubt.
No more fear,
As we are at One
With that Source
That's most dear.

May the Source be with you.

I AM

I am the sound in ether.
I am the air in space.
I am existence everywhere.
I do not have a place.

I am the beauty and the sight,
The fire that lets it be.
I am the water flowing down
Towards my home, the sea.

I am the nourishment of earth;
The roots, the trunk, the leaves.
I am the watching behind mind.
I am that which perceives.

I sound through all that's singing,
The music and the song.
I am the silence behind words.
To Me these all belong.

Unseen behind world's glory.
Unseen behind the mind;
For it is I that's looking;
Though Me you cannot find.

Unless in Meditation,
When mind dwells in My peace,
There in My 'Presence' you will rest
And all else then will cease.

Then in that 'Presence' you will merge.
Then with Me you'll unite.
Beyond all things,
Beyond all thoughts,
Where there's no wrong or right.
Eternal peace,
Eternal rest,
Eternal bliss and light.

The Present

What is the present moment?
What is this time called 'Now'?
Does it proceed from step to step
And if it does, then how?

Do we divide this present
With our minds like skimming stones
Upon the surface of a lake,
Each splash a moment shown?

The water, it is constant,
Though splashes may appear.
Can Time be thus divided
Like points upon a sphere?

Or is it always flowing
Like a river to the sea,
Interrupted by our 'knowing'
When we forget to 'Be'?

Is it measured in our minds
Like ticking hands upon the clock,
That fret their way around its face
Until they finally stop?

So if we stopped the counting,
Ceased punctuating life
With ticks and tocks that actions make
That cause us so much strife?
Would there be – no separate moment
To pass through sequenced time
Of centuries, hours and minutes
Neatly marked along a line?

It's one continuous 'Presence'!
It doesn't have an end
And also no beginning
For all the moments blend
Together in infinity...
We don't know how...
But there is just
'One Great Eternal Now'!

Justice

Justice is what Life just is.
It's constant and it's True.
It's Truth in action;
Truth in speech;
It's in us through and through.
When all our thoughts are silenced,
When our heart is at rest.
This magnifies that 'Presence'
With which all things are blessed.

His Will, it is that Justice
And it will never cease.
His Will is that we show this
In the world as 'His Great Peace'.

Be a Justice of the Peace.

Divine Intelligence

That fine Intelligence,
Constant. Still.
Beyond all acts,
Beyond all will.
Behind the forms
Of me and you
That are so small
In Its wide view.

In that Intelligence
There's no form.
Its silent 'Presence'
From whence we're born,
It watches o'er
From birth to grave
All creatures whether soft or brave.
Unmoved by life's short lows and peaks
It's that we crave,
It's that we seek.
Presiding beyond time and space,
Presiding o'er the human race.
Till finally we come...
Meeting face to face.

Consciousness

Consciousness is everywhere
Projecting on its screen
(That's ever present in our hearts)
This glorious changing scene.
For all this lovely play of life
Experienced within
It's not experienced over there,
If we could hush the din
That's in our minds
We'd know for sure,
We'd know without a doubt,
That there is NOT a 'here' or 'there'.
There's no 'within', there's no 'without'.

This Consciousness is what we are,
Then we'd become aware
That it is us, this Consciousness
And we are everywhere.

Action in Stillness

Action rests in stillness.
The stillness from whence it comes.
We watch as Nature pulls the strings.
It's then that work is fun.

It happens in the moment,
The wide embracing 'Now'.
There is no need to strain and stress
With shoulder to the plough.

To be as little children,
Where everything is play,
Enjoying every moment
From dawn to dusk each day.

There is no yoke to bind us,
Nor burden for to bear.
Each action of this 'Mighty Will'
Is shown to us so clear.
No doubts, desires, aversions.
These finally disperse – and disappear.

Then there is 'art in action',
Life's glorious display.
Our focus it grows finer
And brightens up our way.
Enjoying every moment
Be a child again
Each day!

Devotee! Be Bold!

To practise the 'Presence of God'.
To look at what is most dear.
The desires, anxieties, worries
And especially our fear.
To let these go
So we've been told.
Devotee! Be Bold! Be Bold!

To practise the 'Prayer of Silence'.
That Silence behind all sound.
Forsake all agitation.
Be free! Do not be bound!
So we've been told.
Devotee! Be Bold! Be Bold!

To give up thought of 'other'.
To love the All, the One.
Embracing this vast Universe.
Division! Be there none!
So we've been told.
Devotee! Be Bold! Be Bold!

Unfettered by our actions.
Unfettered by our woes.
Unfettered by relationships.
Unfettered by wealth or gold.
So we've been told.
Devotee! Be Bold! Be Bold!

That 'Presence' is most wonderful.
That 'Presence' is most dear.
That 'Presence' is most lovable.
That 'Presence' is so near.
It's with us on our journey
For all Eternity.
Devotee! Be Bold!
Devotee! Be Bold!
Then clearly you will see
And face to face you'll meet Your Self
To be forever free.

Meditation

I see You in the sky at dawn,
In distant hills and trees.
I hear You in the bird song
That drifts upon the breeze.

I hear You in the Silence
Before the dawn of day,
As sounds of people start to rise,
As they begin the play.

You lie behind those sounds of planes,
Of humming cars and whirring trains.
Again I hear Your call within
And leave behind that busy din.

Then to You I return.
Into that quiet and windless place,
With consciousness come face to face
Where Your flame ever burns.

With consciousness I merge and rest
And in Your heart is my heart blessed.
The two become the One,
As I wait here to greet the morning sun.

The Mantra

The Mantra, it is our best friend
To take us to our journey's end
To rest in the Supreme,
To free us of this dream
Of worldly life
So full of strife.
So it protects us and it will redeem.
That is its goal
And it will free our soul.

To listen to this Godly sound,
To feel its stillness all around.
To feel it move throughout the mind
And in that movement we may find
New depths of subtle peace.
The chatter of our inner voice will cease
And slowly, slowly it will purify
And into deeper depths that lie
Beneath the surface waves of thought
To our True Being we are brought.
That Being which is only One
And then the work of Mantra –
It is done!

Good Company

'Good Company' –
It unifies each soul.
Each one to each,
Each to the 'Infinite Whole'.

It cleanses each of us
From all our past.
It opens up and fills
Each hardened heart
With love and empathy,
Accepting everyone
Without harsh judgement.
Division – there is none.
For we're all children
Underneath God's sun.

Presence

Whose Presence is this that I feel?
It is so constant and so real.
It's penetrating all the show.
It's says "I'm all you need to know",
But without any words.

This Presence with its silent love
It is below,
It is above.
It's all around,
It's through and through.
It's not just me,
It's not just you.
It's everywhere in every place.
It shines its light through every face.

This Presence,
This Intelligence,
Unmoving, gently shines.
It doesn't need to know itself.
It doesn't need a mind.

It is the source of happiness,
The ultimate content.
It is Eternal Comforter,
It is Eternal Friend
Oh Presence,
Please stay close to us
And ncver, never end.

The Eternal Spirit

Mind, meditate on Eternal Spirit.
Heart, offer up all of your soul.
Remember again and again with true reverence
That Ultimate Aim, your goal.

Sight, be aware of who's looking.
Ears, be aware of who hears.
Taste, be aware of who's tasting.
Touch, feel that Presence so near.

Smell, be aware of that Essence,
That Earth which supports through and through.
Senses, bow down to your Maker
Whose elements bind me and you.

Dip your mind into the great ocean
Of Being that is with us each day.
Soak your mind in that sweet constant memory.
Then surrender and enjoy His play.

The Internal Ruler

The Internal Ruler, He moves all this show
Displayed all around and above and below.
His Life lights Mankind with intelligent mind
And thus we can think and can know.

The Internal Ruler resides in our heart
Prompting memory and all that we feel
And whatever we offer to Him with our heart
He receives and then places His seal.

The Internal Ruler is constant and still,
All His powers they move us to perform His Will.
Eternally watching from the depths of His peace,
It is there we can join Him when all movements cease.

The Internal Ruler like the vast ocean deep
Embraces us all as we sink into sleep
And when we awaken to meet the new day,
He is there quietly watching through all this great play.

Published

VERSE

Ryhme and Reason – The Transient

Future Publications

CHILDREN'S PICTURE BOOK AND SHORT STORIES

Bessy Bumble Bee – Picture Book series (7-9 yrs)

The stories of Bessy, a baby bumble bee, meeting and having adventures with the creatures of the English countryside.

Contains first principles for reading and writing in a fun way.

Phoebe: fantasy series for young girls (9-15 yrs)

A young girl goes to sleep and enters a fantasy world.

Based on Josephine's favourite poetry.

Burt the Bionic Bogey series for boys (6-9 yrs)

Story of a young Martian, Burt and his Earth friend, Sam and their adventures around the universe in Burt's rocket space car.

Kepa the Kiwi (7-9 yrs)

Illustrations capturing the colour and character of the birds.

Kepa a young kiwi goes on adventures with the other birds in the New Zealand ancient forests before humans arrived.